Pieces of Me...

by

Duane M. Ward

This book is dedicated to all of the men and women who are living life and looking for love while in the pursuit of happiness. I would like to thank all of my friends and family for your support. A special thanks goes out to Karma for teaching me a valuable lesson and for challenging me to reach my full potential. Without question if it had not been for God, I would not have made it thus far along the way.

Introduction

The secret to success is doing what you love. Well for me this is writing and poetry is one of the gifts or talents that I have. We lose pieces of flesh everyday, revealing a new and improved surface. My compilation of poetry is aptly named Pieces of Me, because each poem reveals a part of me and comes from my soul; revealing my inner thoughts, worries and fears. As a recovering introvert, I have been reluctant to share my most intimate thoughts. Now you have the rare opportunity to see the world through my eyes.

Consider it a privilege to join me on this journey of life, love and the pursuit of happiness. Be forewarned that some of these poems stretch from the deepest emotions of mankind.

In other words, some are censored and some are not. Personally, I think that this makes this book even more unique as many poets and artists only focus on one aspect of life. I see life as art and it's all inclusive. I do not intend to offend anyone, but feel obligated to prepare you to open your hearts and minds to my poetic verse. I thank you in advance. Enjoy.

My Pieces

My Pieces Cont.

Visions

To every individual

They are unique, one of a kind

A picture or thought

Created in one's mind

Just sit and imagine

Anywhere, any place

Travel back in time

Or forward through space

Yesterday

Think of it as the day before

Or call it simply one day ago

To look back some say what for

But some still can't let them go

Yesterday, what did you do?

Where did you go? What did you have on?

Was it a day that slipped past you?

Or did you do something to look back on?

2

Equity

The need
To succeed
The yearn
With a burn

The want
To flaunt
May lead
To greed

Use haste
Avoid waste
To live
One must give

Flowers

First a seed
Then add rain
Soil it will need
To continue the chain

Nitrogen will come
As organisms decay
They take good from
Things thrown away

The sun adds light
The process goes on
Despite the plight
Of being stepped on

Admire the nerve
Of a healthy plant
Air it will serve
Living on what we can't

Reason for the Season

Every three months or so

There occurs a change in the weather

Depending on which direction you go

The forecast may not get better

Do you like it when it's hot or cold?

Some people like it when the air is breezing

Climate can make you feel young or old

Due to the particular month or season

Fantastic Voyage

I would like to thank you
For a very safe trip
As I unfolded and molded
Aboard the "Mother Ship"

Through the many faithful years
Including blood, sweat and tears
Always right by my side
Even though it has not been an easy ride

You have always been there
Like an answer to my prayer
Even when I take it for granted
You help me keep my feet planted

Sometimes I acted like a fool
But you instilled the importance of school
When I went away to acquire more knowledge
You were there to help me pay for college

Now as I go through my mid–life crisis
You are still there, like the Almighty Isis
So before you take your final bow
I want to say, "I love you Mom!"
And give you your flowers now

(Hola Senorita, Unknown)

I saw you sitting there all alone

Looking all gorgeous, just being you

Wanted to talk with you in my bass tone

But I was too shy, didn't know what to do

So I had a sudden urge to leave you a note

And I waited to see some type of sign

That you liked the words that I wrote

As you sat like a bottle of fine wine

To me it was worth the try

To add a little spark to your day

If only a dream to meet you eye to eye

I am just grateful that you came my way

<u>Affection</u>

I want affection

Possibly a love connection

I feel a passion like none before

Could it be the beautiful one that I adore?

Black Beauty

The most beautiful black woman to me

Radiates with natural beauty

Captivating and pleasant brown eyes

To me they have the power to hypnotize

Black and beautiful, two special traits

As she takes care of the home, for her man she waits

Not only black and pretty, but strong willed too

Without a strong black woman, what would a black man do?

Mate Hunting

Watch every step

Don't make any false move

Full of so much pep

Nobody thinks that they can lose

Enjoying the fast life

Living day by day

Avoiding all strife

Nothing getting in your way

Looking for a mate

A task none too easy

You want the love without the hate

Someone sexy, not too sleazy

Watch your step

Never look back

Don't lose your pep

And always avoid the trap!

<u>Anticipation</u>

In my prayer
You were there

I couldn't conceive
That you would ever leave

It made me grin
To see you again

I will hold your hand
For I understand

Its worth the while
To see your pretty smile
And unique style

Broken Glass

Sometimes I am blind
And fail to clearly see
How my lover is so fragile and kind
And my words hurt her so easily

I long to see her bright smile
That livens up my gloomy day
Even if I must be silent for a while
I must try to make a way

Finding ways to show how I feel
Is more meaningful than any word

Determination

Oppression, depression...guilt
Buildings, Nations...built

Fights for rights...earned
Churches, schools...burned

But still we learned!

White is right...instilled
Black blood...spilled

Strong mind, strong willed
Black leaders...killed

"Blacks to the back,"...ended
As legal suits...pended

Blacks lived, died...mourned

As the Civil Rights Movement was born!!

<u>Surprise!</u>

I walk toward an ordinary room

Grab the knob and open the door

I am in the wrong place, the people assume

To myself I ask, "Who were they looking for?"

Did they not know that I was the new recruit?

Was my hair out of place? Did I have a spot on my suit?

I introduce myself, the proper thing to do

One of them smiled and said, "We weren't expecting you..."

Rush Hour

Wake in the morning, can't seem to get it going
Two cups of coffee, yet I'm still yawning

Hop in the shower, got less than a half hour
Gotta punch the clock, because money is power

Jumble through the closet, can't decide what to wear
Running out of time, gotta do something with my hair

Jump in my car running like Batman
On a mission to beat the clock once again

I'm not driving fast, I'm just flying low
But these Sunday drivers are gonna make me blow

So I slow down and take a deep breath
Because making it on time is not worth my death

Survival of the Fittest

It has been said that only the strong survive

If that is the case, then others would be alive

We try to enjoy life, no matter what the cost

Then Bam!..in your face, there's another loss

One step forward, two steps back

Too many choices to stay on the right track

The world of work is full of horrible bosses

You either suck it up, or cut your losses

I

I is just one letter, but so much more
I am the best kept secret and that's for sure
I am way too often misunderstood
I 'm a positive role model with desire to do good

I am a devoted father of a precious one
I am a comedian and love to have fun

I am a teacher of some of the most neglected

I am a professional, highly respected

I am a man still judged by the color of my skin

I am saved, but still tempted by sin

I am blessed with a rich heritage of African, European and

Indian

I am strong, my determination comes from within

I am special, creative and unique

I 'm a work in progress and haven't reached my peak

I am a man on a mission with many goals in store

I is such a small word, but I am so much more

2nd Chances

Rare in this lifetime
Do we receive second chances
Another opportunity
To make further advances

So if it just happens
That you get another try
Nobody but yourself to blame
If you let the occasion pass you by

So make the decision
To right that wrong
Add a few words of encouragement
To the lyrics of that sad song

Put forth the extra effort
And give it all you've got
Take hold of that brass ring
If you get another shot

Rain

Rain

Refreshing, Cool

Irrigating, Invigorating, Rejuvenating

Cascading over the plain

Cleansing, Rinsing, Washing

Silky, Radiant

Rain

What I Miss

I miss the newness of Love
That brand new, never ending feeling
Of happiness...that "puppy love"
Oh how I wish I had that feeling again

The constant attraction
That love connection
Soft hands on my caramel skin
Into her arms I fall, carefree like the wind

At times I lie awake at night
Because it just doesn't feel right
To come in to an empty home
Sleeping in this cold bed alone

I miss the spontaneous hugs
Passionate, soft wet kisses
Quiet whispers of sweet somethings
The chance to make reality out of your secret wishes

Passion

If this world were mine,
We'd be lost in time,
Ever intermingled,
Your spine I'll tingle

I don't care if you're single
Just let me mingle
In your Secret garden
I'll place my hardened tool

There I will work
Like a slave earning his freedom
Committed to your pleasure
My limits have no measure

From here to eternity
I want to spend infinity

I can think of nothing better
As your body gets wetter

You + Me
Equals pure Ecstasy

My Own Worst Enemy

I lie awake at night
Silently contemplating my life
I envision so much more for me
But I must confront my own reality

I am my own worst enemy
For no one has blocked my destiny
It is I who have practiced procrastination
I alone that mentally commits my assassination

My God, My God...what have I done to me
Fascination, infatuation, stagnation
So devil, Get thee behind me
You will no longer hinder my destination

I denounce my sins and claim my soul
No longer under the Satan's mind control
I must stay focused on my destiny
And defeat myself, my own worst enemy

Karma

Karma is a bitch I met one fine day
Never expected her to come around my way
But if you keep living your life on the edge
Eventually U will be stuck by the thorns on the hedge

One night while surfing the world-wide net
I was searching and fishing to see what I could get
Met this fine and sexy tenderonie
So I proceeded to teach her how to ride my little pony

Things were going pretty well I would say
Until I caught her in a lie one unsuspecting day
This was the beginning of my education
As I put in more time and dedication

Karma is seductive, sweet and sexy as hell
Her sex drive and inhibition will put U under a spell
But U better pay attention to the warning signs
She is easily distracted and colors outside the lines

So if u don't have the time to check the facts
Then U might find Karma creeping behind your back
And if U want to have your cake and eat it too
Then Karma will be a bitch and teach U a lesson or two

Poetic Justice

In my mind this is how it should flow

Honesty, loyalty, sprinkled with devotion
Is how a healthy relationship will grow
Tired of the games, the lies and the miss-communication
Trust is earned, this much we all know

I want poetic justice for my time served
I have experienced many things and weathered many storms
At times, I got what I deserved
Other times, been battered and attacked with thorns

I went from living a version of the American dream
To treading water in a shark filled ocean
Can't catch my breath or a break right now it seems
Trying to remix the composition of my love potion
Seems like my nightmare is playing in slow motion

I know that my breakthrough is not far away
But that doesn't eliminate the roadblocks in my path
And I know that the Lord will make a way
But envy and jealousy fuel my wrath
So I must recommit, bow down and pray

As I awake and thank the Lord for a another day
I lay in my bed trying to regain my focus
For I know the enemy will attack me in a new way
So I must surround myself with people of positive substance
For just within my grasp is my Poetic Justice

Final Destination

Every since the dawn of civilization
Man has searched for his salvation
The one who would bear his seed
Make him feel at home and fulfill his needs

Like a mouse seeks out cheese
Man seeks one who makes him weak in the knees
From the mountain on high to the valley low
There are no limits to how far he will go

But when he finds that special one
He must promise to keep her hair and nails done
Take out the trash and mow her lawn
For another man will come along

A true man, knows no limits
And no harm will he permit
He possesses a fascination
To find and secure his Final Destination

The Question of U

What should I say?

What should I do?

To try to solve

The question of U

Where do I go?

And with who?

When all I really want to do

Is to explore the question of U

How to be spontaneous?

Yet extemporaneous

If only I had the manual to

Finally answer the question of U

Could You Be the One?

Could you be the one?

To take my pain away

My ray from the sun

The rainbow on a rainy day

Pondering on the question of me

And the possibility of you

Could you be the one?

The answer is maybe

Now what will you do?

All I Ever Wanted

All I ever wanted was unconditional love;
For God to send me an angel
Created just for me in Heaven above

All I ever wanted was my own private star
To admire it in all its beauty
To always be with me, never far

All I wanted was everlasting kisses
Filled with never ending passion
All I ever got were a few near misses

Once upon a star, thought I found the one in my dreams
Only to realize after 10 years of blood, sweat and tears
Things are not always what they may seem

All I ever needed was to be patient, take my time
Slow down, smell the roses, enjoy the view
For what God has for me, will soon be all mine

28

Are You My Coretta?

Are You my Coretta?
Or Perhaps my Myrlie Evers?
To stand by me through the storm
And work to make this world better

Will you pledge undying love
And stay true to our bond forever?

See, I desire a woman who is
Both strong and quite clever
Loyal to me and down for whatever
Who would leave me only
On the 12th of never

Is this your invitation
Or your notification?
Do you meet the qualifications?
Because if you don't...

I'm still accepting applications

<u>One Wish</u>

If I had one wish

It would simply be

To learn to be more patient

And to enjoy simple beauty

Like the wonders of nature

And the tranquil of the sea

The captured moment of a picture

And the impossible flight of a bee

When the heavens create

We must be still to see

The miracle of birth

And the gift of living eternally

Reality Bites

I crouch down and prepare to fight
I have 9 pit bulls surrounding me ready to bite
All 9 with bone crushing jaws aimed at me
Poised to rip my flesh, they ignore my plea

This is how I feel each day of my life
Living the trials of Job, I lost my home and my wife
Another day, another dollar I owe to someone else
Minute by minute, I lose another piece of myself

But this is my truth, my reality
Work for me is just a formality
My job description gets longer everyday
More paperwork, added responsibility, same pay

I tense up, prepare for flight
As I stare at the 9 pit bulls prepared to bite
Hungry for my blood they salivate
My mortality, my life I contemplate

Is it me or are they closer than before
I search frantically, looking for the back door
Nowhere to run, nowhere to hide
I take a deep breath and swallow my pride

Like a prize fighter realizing he's past his prime
Sensing the urgency, I'm running out of time
I drop to my knees and say the Lord's Prayer
For I know in my heart, He's always there

I raise my head to see a bright light
There are 9 little puppies to my left and my right
My problems were nothing more than a test
To give my life purpose and show how I'm blessed

Hands

One simple gesture can cure mankind
It's not complicated and it's not hard to find

A simple, selfish act everyone understands
The world is at peace when we hold hands

In cities full of crime, the crime rate falls
There's even a reduction in 911 calls

It was simply just amazing to watch
1,000,000 brothers holding hands at the Million Man March

We often forget things that mean so much
Like the therapeutic healing of the human touch

We look for love and someone who understands
There will be peace on earth, when we all hold
Hands

The Rainbow

Just imagine a calming rain

Slowly, gently falling over and over again

Soon followed by a subtle mist

Clouds start to clear as the sun persists

The Sun, the life giving star

Quietly providing light from afar

Silently emerging from its resting place

Perching itself, as if on a throne of grace

Sunlight reaches fresh dew from the shower

Now the chain reaction has reached full power

Creating a full spectrum of vibrant color

Inviting people of all races to love one another

Just in case you didn't know

The power of the rainbow

Summer's Egress

It's really quite amazing to me

That the end of summer will soon be reality

It seems like only yesterday

The heat was chasing the rain away

And when I stop to stand and stare

The flowers of May are no longer there

All too busy enjoying those timeless days

Now the fireworks and barbeques have faded away

As with the passing of a full moon

Those summer memories have gone too soon

34

Sunshine

A beacon of luminescent light
A ray of hope shining so bright
A sudden change in the atmosphere
Occurs when you appear

If only I could make you mine
Sunshine

Mankind contemplates what to do
Just because of you
The way in which you move, defies all laws
Your presence causes mankind to pause

A spectrum of unselfish love
Sent down from the heavens above

Oh, if I could make you mine

Sunshine

Pretty in Pink

My eyes are drawn to a poetic frame
We have a history, so I won't mention her name
The men all pause as she strolls in the room
I try to ignore the aroma of her sweet perfume

I should have known, had I stopped to think
That she would look beautiful, dressed in pink
Soft, subtle, and perfectly curved
Using all my restraint, I control my nerve

I long to tell her that she is still the one
But I am convinced that she has moved on
Oh how long will I feel this way?
Will she ever give me the time of day?

Is it too late to rekindle passions flame?
Or am I doomed to melt at the mention of her name
Maybe I'll just give a simple little wink
Former love of my life, Pretty in Pink

Passion II

I have a never ending passion to be desired
Could it simply be the way I'm hard-wired
I'm a man driven, set out on a quest
Will settle for nothing, nothing less than the best

Like a thunderstorm that's been building for many years
Raindrops forged from a surplus of unused tears
Temporary blindness caused by constant pressure
In search of the right nurse to make it all better

Testosterone and pheromones growing out of control
In need of stimulation of mind, body and soul
Man's inner passion determines how they live
I overflow with a true passion...a passion to give

Little Earthquakes

Tonight is the night..I make you feel like a woman
Succulent candlelight dinner, I cooked just for us two
Fireplace burning, swaying to the quiet storm
We eat, share a laugh and enjoy the oceanic view

As you finish off your chocolate soufflé
I rise, move closer devouring the lure of your perfume
I gently caress your shoulders and ask how was you day
As a cloud of euphoria slowly permeates the room

Slowly kissing the nape of your neck, nibbling your ear
You begin to relax and unwind, I reach out for your hand
You begin to tell me the sweet somethings, I've been dying to
hear
I gently touch your waist as you attempt to stand

Little did you know that I had a master plan
To ease all your tensions, I trace down your seductive frame
I drop to the floor, to show you that I can
Licking the alphabet on your yoni as you scream my name

Circle, circle, I trace figure eights
With a touch of honey, I taste your nectar, the food of the
gods
I aim to erase all your former dates
Strategically placing my fingers to better my odds

You feel the Earth move at the rhythm of my beat
I consume you like a hungry male lion
You thrust your hips into the air, press down with your feet
As my technique, quickly takes you to Zion

I am like Moses, parting the Red Sea
The Earth is trembling, your legs get the shakes
You can't stop the feeling, the oncoming ecstasy
As the table moves, your breath escapes

As you experience
One million tiny earthquakes

An Apple

Ever really looked at an apple?
What did you see?
The vibrant color and simple beauty
Some see the vivacious curves that make
Up one of nature's most unique shapes

Given a second chance
Imagine what you missed
In a hapless glance

First there is the silky, smooth skin
If carefully removed
Will expose the treasured fruit hidden within
Peeling gently over the apple's orbit
To reveal the ample body of delight

Filled with sweet satisfying nectar
Inwardly searching for
The deepest part, known as the core
Its purpose to protect the hibernation
Of the dormant seed
The future of the next generation

Describe an apple, some may say why
But isn't it nice to be
The apple in someone's eye

Strawberries

Strawberries are amazing to me
Craving attention they want the world to see

That they are uniquely created by God above

Show how beautiful they are, so full of love

Engulfed with juices and swollen with pride

A well wrapped package, hiding their present inside

A rough exterior hides the forbidden treasure

A sweet temptation, solely existing for pleasure

Take a moment and examine them up close

The vibrant red color makes you think of a rose

You will also see that they resemble a heart

Why didn't they have you falling in love

From the very start?

Plot

Once upon a time I had a mission
That all started with an exposition
It included the usual suspects
About this, I have no regrets

It just so happened to rhyme
And it all took place in a disclosed location
At a certain point in time

The initiating event had yet to begin
When the main character charged in
There was a conflict with a rival faction
And this led to an eventful rising action

As numerous questions were asked
Finally we reached the climax
This lasted for only a fraction
As we slipped into the falling action

We had to be careful to avoid the smoke screen
As we approached the final scene
And just like a headdress made of exotic feathers
Everything was neatly tied together

By the time we arrived at the resolution

It had all come to a reasonable conclusion

Beauty

Silky, shiny hair blowing radiantly

Shyly hiding what the whole world can see

With a glowing countenance

The look of an angel, pure effervescence

All American, like ice cream and apple pie

A treat to behold, more than meets the eye

Like warm summer rain, pure and simple

With an uplifting smile, complete with dimples

So much more than the cover people see

A treasure to find, a pirate's fantasy

A gift to behold, a real live cutie

Can turn a frown upside down

With her simple beauty

By My Side

I try to make it on my own
You let me know, I'm not alone
You are there when I slip and fall
Without you, there would be no wake up call

You've been right by my side

I remember, 'Footprints in the Sand'
For there stood one doubtful man
Who only saw one set of tracks
Only to realize he rode on your back

You have never left our side

When the storm is rough and the ship is tossed
We must remember, we are not lost
For we are living at God's will
And He can simply say, "Peace be still"

For He is my savior and my guide
And He will never leave my side

Too Intense

This madness of U and Me
My pain so immense
It feels like my heart
Is being ripped out of my chest

U have no idea
The hold U have on me
But do I dare
Ever share
My pain, my agony

For I truly feel
U will wield it as a weapon
To further inflict pain
To my love sick brain
To have it play over again

Further analysis
Could lead to mental paralysis
As the phlebotomist
Nearly goes insane
Trying to find my vein
Using a pick ax

Oh if U could only see
My soul's reality
It would simply be
U + Me

Can't U see
It matters not where
I don't care
But U, the free spirit
Must be in a constant state of flux
Complicating the equation

44

U crave attention from any man
And frankly Scarlet,
I simply will not stand
Idly with my thumb...
Firmly lodged in my ass
As U gaily prance
With your men from France,
Germany or Italy
Behaving STUPIDLY

Detained

Once upon a time while minding my own

Came a knock at the door from a source unknown

Not sure who it was in the middle of the night

I threw on some pants and turned on the light

To my surprise it was a clone of Barney Fife

Who asked some questions about my personal life

I answered freely to gain an understanding

Until the officer became demanding

I was kindly asked to ride to the station

Shocked and surprised about the current situation

Should I call someone and let them know?

Or cooperate and hope they let me go

I decided to wait and see

As I rode in the back like a refugee

When I arrived I was placed in handcuffs

I grew tired of this bad dream, I had enough

He further explained the procedure

As I sat in a chair looking beleaguered

I had to talk to the magistrate

For he held the key to my ultimate fate

Elephants in My Yard

You may say that it is all a facade

But I grew up with elephants in my yard

Fiercely through the jungle, they did not roam

Instead they stood watch over my childhood home

Majestically ever reaching towards the endless sky

Like the immortal Titans, you can not beat them if you try

With their seemingly impenetrable, pale gray skin

They harbor tremendous power hidden deep within

Though they howled and screamed at the top of their lungs

And threw branches at us with their limbs as they swung

They gifted my family with their life giving breath

And will be with my descendents, until they face a slow death

I am truly blessed to have been under their protection

Shading me from the sun, they showed their affection

Proudly guarding my parent's home, they still stand guard

I am forever indebted to the Elephants in my yard

Missing You

How do I miss thee?

Let me see

Like a camel

Misses his hump

Like a log

Misses its stump

Like a river

That doesn't give a dam

Like Sam I Am

Missed Green Eggs and Ham

Like pollen

Misses a bee

But I wonder though...

Do you miss me?

Phenomenal

At first glance, couldn't believe my eyes

All that style, such a welcomed surprise

Poetry in motion, such style and grace

Leaving trails of happiness all over this place

One can't help, but smile and say hi

Like a refreshing summer breeze, when you pass by

Like a kid on Christmas, just can't wait

Until you pass my way again, I anxiously wait

Reflections

As I reflect into the deepest regions of my mind

My thoughts seem to be lost, no concern for time

The complete anthology of all my hopes and dreams

Are stored there in Pandora's box, bursting at the seams

What shall become of my greatest aspirations

My hopes for tomorrow, my latest temptations

Did I choose wisely in my last adventurous quest

Or did I come up one question short on a crucial test

Just wishful thinking as I search to find

The moral to my story, Lord send me a sign

So I relax and breathe deeply, relaxing my mind

For all questions will be answered in their own sweet time

21 Questions

If I were hurt, would you really care?
Or would you make excuses, why you couldn't be there?
If I committed a crime would you turn me in?
If I lost my apartment, would you take me in?

Would you choose your friends over me?
With me would you share all your fantasies?

Could you count every one of my 1000 kisses?
What would you ask for, if I gave you 3 wishes?
What would you say your favorite dish is?
How about if I asked you to be my mistress?

Could you stand if I licked the ABC's on your yoni?
Would you perform tricks on my little pony?
If I were sick, would you nurse me better?
Would you tell me what makes you wetter?

Would you make love with me in the rain?

Do you enjoy the contrast of pleasure and pain?

What is your secret recurring dream?

Can you be creative, with strawberries and whipped cream?

Would you prefer to make love over sex?

Do you seek the one who treats you best?

True love is so hard to find
Would you feel free to bare
What's on your beautiful mind?

A Taste of Chocolate

More frequently I have had a craving

For a sweet indulgence that all are raving

A flavor so rich, it's the ultimate

I have a fever for a taste of chocolate

Driving alone, one suddenly misses

Still remember those pure Hersey's Kisses

Closer and closer I try to get

Just have to satisfy my hunger

For a taste of chocolate

Strawberries II (uncensored)

Imagine nature's perfect fruit

That you can play with in your birthday suit

Seductively curved and shaped like a heart

Tempting and daring you to tear them apart

Strawberries on top of me

Could be nothing short of ecstasy

Sweet red juices dripping over my skin

Ravenous tongues licking, feels like a sin

I grow impatient waiting for the season to begin

And for all the adventures strawberries and I will be in

Never underestimate the simple treasure

Where you can find life's ultimate pleasure

Honey

Let's start with a substance
With just the right texture
Yet sweet enough
To supply endless pleasure

A taste so full of flavor
That you will never forget
Your senses will savor
All the honey you can get

Where can you find this sweet treat?
At your local food store
On shelves nice and neat

But what is it used for?

You can use it on biscuits, waffles or toast
On pancakes or anything made of bread
But where could it be utilized most?
To answer this, one must use their head

Think of all the sticky situations
That one could create
When you give into sweet temptations
Oh the many desserts, lovers can create

That Smile

Ever notice that unusual glow

The one that you haven't seen in quite a while

But when you witness it you instantly know

The moment you see a face with That Smile

Some may not know just what I mean

Because they have yet to encounter that special look

You might mistake it for an ad in a high profile magazine

But That Smile is so unique, simply off the hook

First time I noticed, it was just a passing glance

Taking for granted the elated expression

But then I observed their glowing countenance

And I learned a most valuable lesson

I immediately knew why I became so envious

As I had witnessed the most remarkable afterglow

A person so consumed by a passion, so mysterious

When you look at them it will always show

A smile so wide, it stretches from ear to ear

So intense, nothing else seems to matter

No worries, no cares, concerns or fear

One might even say they have a certain swagger

As nothing else in the world seems to matter

So now to explain this new form of ecstasy

You have to envision the morning after birthday sex

Naturally simplistic and totally stress free

Not even the least concerned with what happens next

And the next time you see a person with "that" look

Just know that if they were in the jaws of a crocodile

They would still be able to write a 500 page book

Describing the intimate sexual healing of

That Smile

The Sundress

I couldn't have imagined a hotter day
Like a dream she appeared, walking my way
Frozen with excitement, not sure what to do
I took in the full unadulterated view

Like Marilyn Monroe when dressed in white
Her natural form was one amazing sight
It may not have been her intention to impress
But every man's jaw dropped at the sight of that sundress

Her hair flowed like fine imported silk
And she had smooth caramel skin, like chocolate milk
With muscle tone as tight as strings on a harp
She had the legs of a sprinter and that set her apart

Her most astonishing feature to me
Was that she never seemed to notice all the activity
Yet her body moved like the waves of the ocean
Like she was mixing her own natural love potion

As I watched with reckless abandon
A strange thing started to happen
The wind suddenly turned into a swift breeze
And my sinful thoughts brought me to my knees

Like James Brown singing "Please...Please...Please!"
I had one simple request for this gentle breeze
That wish I am happy to confess
Was that that wind would somehow find
The hem of that sundress

Pieces of Me

I may percolate, simmer or boil

But my feet remain firmly planted in the soil

So much more than most people ever see

For my poetry reveals tiny pieces of me

Forged from a unique ancestral past

At times in life I've been treated like an outcast

So much determination, strength and pride

My talents continue to grow, too many to hide

At an early age I formulated a plan

To put words into print so others may understand

Many think that I have to rehearse

But I can transform any word into verse

Some say this is a gift and others a curse

I can think of several afflictions that are much worse

Many people try to sing, some like to dance

I like to dabble in the art of lyrical romance

58

If I had to be a plant, I would be a tree

As an insect I'd "float like a butterfly and sting like a bee"

Let my voice be heard as I go down in history

My anthologies of poetry are "pieces of me"

Yoni

The origin of life
My secret hiding place
The rose petals of a wife
Each one so unique and soft as lace

But I search for only one
The one made just for me
It will melt on my tongue
And show me the path to ecstasy

It will be my desert oasis
My favorite vacation destination
Taking my mind to so many special places
Thinking of my yoni, my mind races

When I taste the sweet nectar
Time does not exist
Cascading like a flooded river
Causing a flood of endless bliss

60

Dante's Peak

Secretly waiting for the right moment since birth
Like a giant cicada buried deep in the Earth
Activated by the movement of tectonic plates
Deep in the Earth's core my breakthrough awaits

Held down for so long and never really noticed
Can't wait to awaken like a swarm of locusts
Nothing as potent has been witnessed before
Like the birth of an island from a distant shore

Temperature rising like the La Brea tar pits
This force of nature is as hot as it gets
Like an ancient pyramid hiding a Pharaoh's treasure
A gift to the world, too priceless to measure

The chance of a lifetime is finally here
Crowds gather to see from far and near
Too much time has passed for stage fright
Headed straight to the top for the timing is right

Approaching the summit, otherwise known as the climax
Takes all of my composure to simply relax
Finally daylight appears as I touch the sky
My peak bursts through causing boulders fly

Those Eyes

As I reminisce about your misadventures and lies
I can never forget the distinctive look of your eyes
If a man truly knows you, he'll know where to find
Exactly what's on your beautiful mind

If given a choice of what I'd wake up to see
Looking into your beautiful eyes is what it would be
Big, beautiful and open wide
Uniquely shaped even with no makeup applied

Your eyes really are the window of your soul
And when you look at me, I feel made whole
As time goes on and days go by
I still long to be the apple of your eye

Though the reality is I can never be
The only man you desire to see
So you scour the Earth seeking your prize
I am envious of the man who captures those eyes

62

Moving On

Still remember the day we first met
The cards were stacked and the deal was set
Filled with butterflies not knowing what to expect
Your wish was my command and your honor I'd respect

Routine phone calls lasting all night long
Thought I had it all right, but maybe I was all wrong
Random text in the middle of the day
Your seductive words made me feel some type of way

Couldn't wait to have you all alone
So we could do all we had said on the phone
A feeling of newness, my forbidden love
Still when I fantasize, it's you I think of

Its been a year now, time went so fast
In the back of my mind, I knew it wouldn't last
Do we really have to part this way?
Or could we reminisce for one endless day

And now I sit alone every night
Thinking of you and it doesn't feel right
Trying not to imagine who's holding you now
But I guess it's my turn to take a bow

I know that I'll find love again one day
But that doesn't take the any of the sting away
You are a diamond in the rough that I stumbled upon
The day seems a little darker now, but I must move on

A New Day

Thunder roared and lightning flashed
Throughout the nighttime thunderstorm
A new day is dawning the nightmare has passed
Sunlight is spreading, the air is so warm

At times I doubted that everything would be alright
As the rain slammed down and the wind blew fast
Things got rough and the storm raged all night
But God don't like ugly and this too shall pass

Had to relax my mind and say a prayer
For I know my God is always there
Trouble may come and darken the night
But joy comes in the morning
And the new day shines bright

Inside

As I awake and take my first breath
I think about how much time I have left
Here on God's green Earth
I've learned to value a woman's worth

Isn't it ironic the strange things people say
Many make no sense, others are just so cliché
But I can say with confidence and pride
There is no place I'd rather be than inside

Inside of what many may stop and ask
A place like no other...a comfort zone
Where nothing else matters and time doesn't exist
Many see a glimpse of heaven inside of this

This thing that has a strange name
Can leave one obsessed craving it over and over again
So pace yourself and swallow your pride
Meditation helps you relax when you come inside

Like a glove lined with the finest silk
With fountains of ambrosia, honey and milk
I can't imagine a more perfect place to hide
Than the tunnel of love waiting inside

A Mile In Your Shoes

Whether traveled by country road or city street
A mile equals five thousand, two hundred and eighty feet
Step by step we leave our unique tracks
With our future to face and our past at our backs

When meeting someone, show a little empathy
Because they just might need our sympathy
Life for them may not have been a crystal stair
We may never know, because we were not there

And we might have a dark past of our own
Some skeletons in our closet are better left alone
So before you throw that first stone
Just know like a boomerang, it will find its way home

So no matter your position or your wealth
Consider one's feelings or current state of health
Before you lash out like you have nothing to lose
Take a moment and walk a mile in their shoes

Epiphany

A wise person said, success is living your dreams
Another, the grass is not always as green as it seems
I want to orchestrate my life just like a symphony
A mind is like a well designed clock waiting for that epiphany

So take care of yourself and order your steps
Keep your feet still and they will get swept
Stay alert and constantly feed your mind
The sky is the limit for the gifted mankind

You are what you eat and become what you think
So watch your diet and don't let your ship sink
We must study our craft and feed our brains
Or our minds will grow too weak to break these chains

If you stop working out, your muscles turn soft
So don't sit in the dark with the light turned off
Get started today writing your life symphony
And prepare yourself for that great epiphany

Meet the Author: Duane M. Ward

He was born in Richmond, VA and attended Middlesex Public Schools. An honor graduate of Virginia State University, he earned his bachelor's degree in Public Administration and served as vice president of that academic club. His "real talk" style of writing was first noticed by his 11th grade English teacher and honed throughout his college and personal life. Now nearly 40 years later, Duane is ready to share his life experiences in written form.

He was blessed with a wonderful daughter who often pulls on his heart string. Family is important as well as leaving the world a better place than when we entered it. Poetry is only one outlet and writing in general is his passion. Duane enjoys nature, museums and the simple pleasures in life; and is currently debating which is more beautiful the sunset or the sunrise. "The sunrise seems to have the edge, because if you see it that means you have been blessed with another day." Duane M. Ward(1966-)